Beatrix & Peter Rabbit

A CENTENARY CELEBRATION FROM THE COLLECTIONS OF GROLIER CLUB MEMBERS

New York

THE GROLIER CLUB

15 NOVEMBER 2001 TO 11 JANUARY 2002

THE GROLIER CLUB
47 EAST 60TH STREET
NEW YORK, N.Y. 10022

ISBN 0-910672-39-3

1500 copies printed by the Ascensius Press

PREFACE

December 2001 marked the hundredth anniversary of *The Tale of Peter Rabbit,* one of the most popular children's books of all time. Beatrix Potter's story and its accompanying illustrations, introduced with the familiar words "Once upon a time there were four little Rabbits, and their names were—Flopsy, Mopsy, Cottontail, and Peter," as well as the later tales in the Peter Rabbit series, have been delighting readers of all ages for the past century.

To honor Peter's first appearance in print, the Grolier Club held the exhibition recorded in these pages. Since the show was organized under the auspices of the Club's Committee on Prints, Drawings, and Photographs, the emphasis was on original artworks, with a representative sampling of books, manuscripts, and autograph letters. Early on it was decided to limit the items (with two exceptions) to those produced during Potter's lifetime. To do otherwise was foolish; the array of Potteriana and Peteralia—later editions, piracies, knockoffs, parodies, toys, merchandise, *stuff*— is so vast that even a fraction of what is available would fill the exhibition space of a major museum, never mind the Rare Book Room of the Grolier Club. But even after identifying the kind of items wanted, making a choice proved difficult. It turned out that among the membership of the Club there are a handful of dedicated Potter fans (and others for whom Potter is a side-interest) who own more wonderful material than could be displayed. Who would have imagined that the final selection for an exhibition drawn entirely from private collections might include not just inscribed copies of the first three editions of *The Tale of Peter Rabbit*, but also illustrated letters to Eric and Noel Moore (for whom the story was written), and an original Peter Rabbit doll, made for Potter herself? Add to these riches the autograph manuscript of *The Story of a Fierce Bad Rabbit;* working drawings for *The Pie and the Patty-Pan;* two of Potter's rare "toy pictures"; the earliest known version of "Cecily Parsley"; and splendid watercolors depicting flora, fauna, fairy tales, and imaginary doings in the animal world, and the result was a unique opportunity for members and public alike to see the timeless beauty and ingenuity of the artwork and writing of Beatrix Potter.

Members' exhibitions at the Grolier Club are, by their nature, collaborative efforts. In putting together "Beatrix Potter & Peter Rabbit" I was helped, first and foremost, by my marvelous co-curators, Justin C. Schiller and Mary K. Young. They deserve the multi-carrot medal (with lettuce leaf clusters) for services beyond the call of duty. Justin's knowledge of "who owns what" proved invaluable, and he aided in distilling the long list of potential loans into a manageable and cohesive form; moreover, he made available, often on short notice, his own and his firm's extensive Potter expertise derived from decades of handling her works. Mary not only cheerfully took on the job of installing the show (to perfection), but dealt, in the absence of a registrar, with loan details and security arrangements; she even lent me her precious copy of Quinby's rare bibliography, so essential for writing about Potter's books. My gratitude goes also to the Grolier staff, notably Director-Librarian Eric Holzenberg and Administrative Assistant

Maev Brennan; to our former Registrar, Nancy Houghton; and to the following: William H. Helfand, Linda Lear, Carol Z. Rothkopf, Mary C. Schlosser, Arthur L. Schwarz, Jean Stephenson, Margaret D. Stetz, Jill Tarlau, and Tony Yablon. Andrea Immel, Curator of the Cotsen Children's Library, Princeton University, and her West Coast counterpart, Ivy Trent, Personal Librarian of Lloyd E. Cotsen, greatly facilitated the selection and transport of materials owned by Mr. Cotsen. Marilyn Barth, perceptive and astonishingly adept at bibliographic research, made complexities simple and did much of the work on the labels; without her the exhibition might never have come off. Finally—and most importantly—I wish to thank those Grolier members who generously allowed the Club to borrow, for a while, treasured Potter from their shelves and walls. The lenders included Lloyd E. Cotsen, David J. Holmes, Cecily Langdale Davis, Edward R. Leahy, David R. Macdonald, Arthur L. Schwarz, Justin C. Schiller, Betsy B. Shirley, and Mary K. Young.

MARK SAMUELS LASNER
Chair, Committee on Prints, Drawings, and Photographs

BEATRIX POTTER
AND AESTHETICISM

"Some critics say," as Wilfred M. Leadman wrote in a judicious and sympathetic article for *The Westminster Review* of 1906, that this "art may be very entertaining and very clever," but that it is mere "ornament." Yet, Leadman asserted, many British readers felt that it "helped them to realise the wonder of much that previously seemed common and graceless." It was, moreover, work that "bristles with moral advice" and a "stern moral lesson," while being an "irresistible overflow of an ever creative intellect."

The art in question was not by Beatrix Potter, but by Oscar Wilde, yet Leadman's remarks could have applied to either. Linking these two names now helps us to recognize their kinship, as the two figures from the turn of the century who most influenced and dominated twentieth-century culture. No one else of their day in England produced art that had such a great and continuing impact around the globe through its translation into numerous languages or that reached both children and adults, inspired so many reissues, copies, parodies, and interpretations in different media, fuelled social and political movements (from environmental conservation in one case to gay rights in the other), and attracted such devoted cult followings. Wilde and Potter even shared subject matter, for the talking animals with their all-too-human foibles that populated Wilde's fairy tales of the 1880s were surely important antecedents for the denizens of Potter's world.

December 2000 saw the one-hundredth anniversary of Oscar Wilde's death, with an accompanying flurry of reflection and appreciation. The year 2001 is the centenary of the issue of Potter's *The Tale of Peter Rabbit*. There may be more links between these events than at first appear, for surely no adult reader in 1901 who encountered Potter's little book—an expanded version of her illustrated letter to Noel Moore from September 1893—could have received its story of a disobedient creature in a dandified blue jacket and shiny shoes who breaks the rules for rabbits, crosses a boundary to indulge himself, and pays for his recklessness with imprisonment, disgrace, and even the loss of his distinctive costume without hearing what Wilfred Leadman might have called a "stern moral lesson" that resonated beyond the animal world.

Beatrix Potter's journals record her first sighting of Wilde and the visual impression he left some ten years before his trials and incarceration: "He is not peculiar as far as I noticed," she wrote in 1885, "rather a fine looking gentleman, but inclined to stoutness." The occasion was a visit each made separately to an exhibition at the gallery of the Fine Art Society. But they could have observed one another on numerous occasions, for both frequented shows of contemporary art, especially at the Grosvenor Gallery. This was the venue which became so notorious for welcoming work by artists of the Aesthetic movement that W. S. Gilbert immortalized it as such in his 1881 libretto for *Patience*, an operetta satirizing Aestheticism. Wilde was a champion of such painters; Potter was anything but. Her deep streak of conservatism (which later made her a passionate advocate for the conservation of nature and preservation of English rural life) informed not only her moral but artistic judgment. Echoing Gilbert's *Patience*, she railed in 1884, "As for the greenery yallery Grosvenor Gallery painters, they *is* [*sic;* her emphasis] there in full force, as contemptible as ever." Potter's journals would demonstrate that this was no fleeting opinion, for her commentary upon works by the likes of Edward Burne-Jones was consistently vitriolic.

Yet if the Wilde of *Dorian Gray* was torn between amorality and an equally strong preference for "stern" moralism, so, too, was Beatrix Potter complex and contradictory, not singleminded, in her tastes and allegiances. Her biographer, Judy Taylor, has emphasized the impact on Potter of her long friendship with John Everett Millais, whose studio she visited often. Millais, a founder of the Pre-Raphaelite Brotherhood, was also a friend to Burne-Jones and to many of the artists from whose work she initially recoiled. His influence encouraged her to reconsider her first impressions and to try to discern what might be worth studying.

From the Pre-Raphaelites, Potter learned to be a precise recorder of natural detail. But from the Aesthetes' Japanese-influenced ideals of simplicity, asymmetry, and deployment of empty space in the composition, she also acquired much. Scenes of nature in volumes such as *The Tale of Squirrel Nutkin* (1903) and *The Story of a Fierce Bad Rabbit* (1906) showed a Pre-Raphaelite's attention to foreground detail, yet sometimes left backgrounds sketchily impressionistic and suggestive in a way that would have pleased even J. M. Whistler. That she could draw (not to pun) from work she claimed to despise is clear. So is her unacknowledged affinity with the Aesthetes disclosed by her penchant for holding antithetical principles in a delicate and unresolved tension, her preference for the dress and styles of what W. S. Gilbert would mock as "the reign of Good Queen Anne," and her interest in making beautiful what might at first seem strange, violent, or shocking.

The popular image in past years has been of Potter as a sheltered and repressed young woman, connecting with the world only through her animal friends—an image that grew out of anti-Victorian, misogynist stereotypes circulating during much of the twentieth century. To portray young women such as Beatrix Potter as lost in a dream or as held sternly in check by ridiculous proprieties was just another way for the recently ended century to distinguish itself from the one before and to clap itself on the back for its own supposed liberation. But the distorted picture of Beatrix Potter as a girl locked away in a tower, with only her cottontailed confidantes, bears as little relation to her life of active cultural engagement and learning as it does to the lives of most of Potter's late-Victorian peers, including her contemporaries, the feminist "New Women" of the 1890s.

What her journals, as transcribed by Leslie Linder, demonstrate is that Potter was in the thick of the English art scene of the 1880s, while in her teens and twenties. Her visits to the Royal Academy and to shows in the salerooms at Christie's, as well as to the Grosvenor Gallery and the Fine Art Society, were frequent. She kept detailed records of which pictures she saw, how she felt about them, and what she gleaned about technique and style, while forming her artistic tastes. Although she was living under the parental roof, these tastes were her own and sometimes quite different from those of her father, a dedicated amateur photographer. When, in 1883, Rupert Potter brought home a copy of John Ruskin's *Modern Painters* with "Mr. Ruskin's autograph on the title page, stating he gave the book to D. G. Rossetti," the seventeen-year-old Beatrix dismissed the "curious" purchase, writing, "Interesting copy, not that I think much of either chappy."

Her opinions could be devastating. Of Burne-Jones's paintings, on view in 1886, she wrote with a nineteen-year-old's self-confidence that they were "very weak in drawing, morbid in style, and forced and ridiculous in sentiment." At the same time, her developing artist's eye compelled her to acknowledge that there might be something there worth a second look, especially in "the panels of creation" (*The Days of Creation*, 1872–76), with their "harmonious combinations of blues and greys." Indeed, she carefully and thoughtfully studied canvases by the Pre-Raphaelites and their successors, the Aesthetic painters, on numerous occasions in the 1880s. An 1886 visit, for instance, to the Grosvenor Gallery's retrospective of work by Millais occasioned a meditation with consequences for her later work. She wrote:

Examine the focus in *Ferdinand* [*Ferdinand Lured by Ariel*, 1849], it is a marvel of perfection in drawing, and, I affirm, in colour; but the absence of shadow, which would obscure parts, renders it muddy. . . . perhaps focus is the real essence of pre-Raphaelite art. . . . Everything in focus at once, which though natural in the different planes of the picture, produces on the whole a different impression from that which we receive from nature. Which method is right, all in focus or only one plane, is an open question.

That she absorbed and took instruction from this became obvious years afterward; in "The Veal and Ham Pie," for instance, from her 1905 *The Pie and the Patty-Pan*, Duchess the dog stands on a stone path framed by plants and tall flowers—every blossom in clear focus, with those farthest from the spectator just as detailed as those nearest.

The pattern of her approach to the Pre-Raphaelites—i.e., out-of-hand dismissal, followed by reconsideration and, later still, by judicious borrowing—was doubly true with the Aesthetes. In 1883, she wrote mockingly that "Mr. Whistler is holding an Exhibition somewhere, termed an *Arrangement in white and yellow.* The furniture is painted yellow and the footman is dressed in white and yellow, someone said he looked like a poached egg. Mr. Whistler sent the Princess of Wales and the fine ladies yellow butterflies which they wore at the private view. What a set of yellow butterflies! It's quite disgusting how people go on about these Pre-Raphaelite aesthetic painters." It was plain that she was going on secondhand reports, probably from the newspapers, which were hostile to the American upstart who had won the notorious libel case against Ruskin. Nonetheless, she would produce her own wash of yellow-and-white twenty years later, in *The Tailor of Gloucester* (1903), where the tiny head of the tailor in bed is a minor element, dominated by the yellow bedcurtains and white counterpane, which fill the eye with aesthetic drapery. In her own works, too, she would employ the kinds of flat planes and asymmetrical compositions of Japanese woodblock prints that had influenced Whistler. A striking example is the image from *The Tale of Mrs. Tittlemouse* (1910) which places the ladybug, looking as though she were kimono-clad, in the lower foreground and the mouse diagonally upper-left, both figures enclosed in an off-center oval frame of foliage and earth. Here and in other books, such as *The Tale of Mrs. Tiggy-Winkle* (1905), Potter would also experiment with such Japanese-cum-British-aesthetic effects as the use of roundels, rather than images of rectangular shape.

At times, the prose in which Potter records her own artistic pronouncements smacks of hand-me-down Aestheticism or perhaps Wilde-and-water. She rhapsodizes, in 1886, that "Nature . . . is made of colour. There is no such thing as its absence. It shows the work of one who understood that perfection is beauty. What we call the highest and lowest in nature are both equally perfect. A willow bush is as beautiful as the *human form divine*." By then, she certainly would have read newspaper accounts of Wilde's lectures. Even before seeing him in 1885, she was aware of and interested in him, recording her parents' 1884 meeting with Wilde at "a Ball at the Millais' . . . . [where] He was not wearing a lily in his button hole, but, to make up for it, his wife had her front covered with great water-lilies." The doctrine that there was no such thing as high or low in art, merely The Beautiful, was certainly his. It became hers, as well, when she began to draw the lowest of creatures—crows and toads, mice and lizards, beetles and little cottontails—as specimens of perfection and beauty. We might say that Potter's subjects are Wilde rabbits, as well as wild ones.

Like the Aesthetes, too, she was fascinated by costume and especially taken with fashions of the previous century. In the first illustration for her 1903 *The Tailor of Gloucestor*, the Lord Mayor and his lady in eighteenth-century finery seem to have stepped straight off a painted silk fan of the 1890s by Charles Conder. So, too, the deliciously ornate portrait from the same volume of "A Little Lady Mouse," in ruffles and hoops, owes much to Aubrey Beardsley's 1896 edition of *The Rape of the Lock*—a debt confirmed by the reference to the sly voyeurism that was a hallmark of Beardsley's drawings (though here, the eyes of the otherwise concealed observer belong only to another mouse). To read *The Tailor of Gloucester*, moreover, is to feel one has come across a lost chapter of *The Picture of Dorian Gray*, or perhaps a lost parody of Chapter Eleven, the one with catalogues of Dorian's treasures, including his choice embroideries: "[The] tailor began to make a coat—a coat of cherry-coloured corded silk embroidered with pansies and roses, and a cream-coloured satin waistcoat—trimmed with gauze and green worsted chenille. . . ."

From the Aesthetes, too, Potter absorbed the doctrine that beauty required not regularity, but strangeness, a concept made famous by Walter Pater in the 1880s and circulated in the popular press. In the case of Beatrix Potter's art, the strangeness came from the combination of elegant, dandified clothing or daintily furnished interiors and the bodies of furry, scaled, or feathered animals with dangerous teeth, beaks, and claws—an unsettling and almost perverse way of commenting upon the unnatural through the natural, and vice versa, that the Decadents might have appreciated, if they had lived past 1900 (the year that saw the death of Wilde, as one of the last of their number). There was, indeed, something perverse about Potter herself, respectable and down-to-earth as she always seemed in public. In a journal entry for 1890, she records what can only be called an erotic dream about her rabbit, Benjamin Bouncer. The episode begins with a celebration of having sold to a publisher some greeting cards featuring Benjamin's likeness. Like a practiced seducer, she drugs the rabbit with

> a cupful of hemp seeds, the consequence being that when I wanted to draw him next morning he was partially intoxicated and wholly unmanageable. Then I retired to bed, and lay awake chuckling till 2 in the morning, and afterwards had the impression that Bunny came to my bedside in a white cotton night cap and tickled me with his whiskers.

The implications of this image are unmistakable: years before Oscar Wilde was pilloried for The Love That Dare Not Speak Its Name, Beatrix Potter had known The Love That Dare Not *Squeak* Its Name.

Potter and Wilde—the names are seldom found together in histories of turn-of-the-century literature and art, yet both figures can be appreciated now as defining spirits. Neither had a reputation that was expected to last or, of course, to spread so widely in such diverse directions. The supposedly great artists of their generation—who knows their works now? But Potter and Wilde, accused of being frivolous, trivial, and insufficiently serious in their styles or choices of subject, are with us forever. So, too, are their immortal, fantastical creations: a beautiful, headstrong youth known as "Dorian" and, of course, a beautiful, headstrong rabbit known as "Peter."

MARGARET D. STETZ
Associate Professor of English and Women's Studies
Georgetown University

CATALOGUE OF THE EXHIBITION

NATURAL HISTORY

Beatrix Potter's interest in drawing began when she was a child. Her talent was encouraged by both her parents, but especially by her father, a gifted photographer and amateur artist who took her to exhibitions at the Royal Academy and arranged for art lessons. She was a keen observer of the natural world, both with her naked eye and through the lens of a microscope. Her remarkable paintings and drawings of flora and fauna were the result of careful studies made in the gardens and countryside she visited on family holidays in England and Scotland.

1. *Agaraicus xerampelinus va 5.* Watercolor, [ca. 1893–1898).

Mushrooms captivated Potter, who became a serious student of mycology and between 1883 and 1901 made hundreds of paintings and microscopic drawings, most of which she later donated to the Armitt Library in Ambleside. Her intensive research resulted in a paper, "On the Germination of the Spores of Agaricineae," that was read before the Linnean Society on 1 April 1897 by a man—women not being allowed to be present. Potter hoped that her paintings of fungi would be published, but it was not until 1967, over twenty years after her death, that fifty-nine of them were used as illustrations for W. P. K. Findlay's *Wayside and Woodland Fungi.*

2. *Flower Study.* Watercolor, 1886.

Potter was twenty when she made this watercolor of geraniums at Camfield Place, the Hertfordshire home of her grandfather, Edward Potter. She presented it to her governess, Miss Hammond, who encouraged her artistic activities.

3. *Study of the Head of a Bat, in Right Profile.* Watercolor, October 1888.

This may depict the bat which Potter's brother Bertram kept as a pet. "It is a charming little creature," she wrote, "quite tame and apparently happy as long as it has sufficient flies and raw meat."

4. *Studies of Fish.* Watercolor, October 1884.

In the month she drew these fish, Potter wrote in her *Journal:* "It is all the same, drawing, painting, modelling, the irresistible desire to copy any beautiful object which strikes the eye. Why cannot one be content to look at it? I cannot rest, I must draw, however poor the result, and when I have a bad time come over me it is a stronger desire than ever and settles on the queerest things . . . ."

5. *Studies of Mice.* Watercolor, October 1890.

"I had many mouse friends in my youth," Potter recalled late in life, "I was always catching and taming mice; the common wild ones are far more intelligent and amusing than the fancy variety, but strange to say mine never bred in spite of having much liberty and comfortable neat boxes."

6. *Mouse in its Nest.* Oil on board, [ca 1891–1892].

At age seventeen Potter began a series of twelve art lessons, taught by an unidentified "Mrs. A," with whom she studied oil painting. Only a few oils attributed to Beatrix Potter are known. This painting of a mouse in its nest was given in 1944 by Potter's husband, William Heelis, to her first biographer, Margaret Lane.

7. *Greeting Card with Two Mice.* London: Hildesheimer and Faulkner, [1890].

In May 1890, in an act she described to her father as one of "pique and the desire for coin," Potter made her first move to get her artwork published. Her initial step was to send six Christmas cards (featuring her pet rabbit Benjamin) to the firm of Marcus Ward, who rejected them. With the help of her brother and her uncle, Sir Henry Roscoe, she then approached Hildesheimer and Faulkner, specialists in greeting cards and gift books. This time, to her amazement, she received payment of £6 by return mail— and a request for more designs, of which this chromolithographed card is an early example.

8. *Fawe Park Garden.* Watercolor, 1903.

In the summer of 1903, the Potter family stayed at Fawe Park, a large house on the shores of Derwentwater, near Lingholm in the Lake District. It was here that Beatrix Potter worked on *The Tale of Benjamin Bunny*, the sequel to *Peter Rabbit*. The garden served, she told Norman Warne, as the site for "every imaginable rabbit background" and the subject of many "miscellaneous sketches." This "sketch," in fact a highly finished work in the British watercolor tradition, incorporates in the foreground a sleeping cat which resembles the one which, in the story, is chased away by Old Mr. Bunny.

RABBITS OF THE 1890S

Of all Potter's pets—and these included mice, hedgehogs, lizards, turtles, and snakes—the ones which meant the most to her were her rabbits. She had two, both Belgian males: Benjamin (known as Benjamin Bunny, Benjamin Bouncer, Mr. Benjamin H. Bouncer, or just plain "Bounce") and his successor, Peter (also called Peter Piper). Benjamin and Peter, who were both "capable of developing strong character," served as a continuous inspiration for Potter in the 1890s. She depicted them *au naturel* and also anthropomorphized, clothed and acting as humans.

9. *Rabbits, Apple Picking.* Ink over pencil, [ca. 1890s].

Here Peter Rabbit and one of his brothers are seen gathering apples. Peter is in his coat, pushing a wheelbarrow, while the brother, wearing an apron with a basket slung over his right shoulder, holds a walking stick in his left paw.

10. *Two Rabbits Gathering Apples.* Ink, with traces of pencil, [ca 1893].

11. *Study of Two Rabbits.* Ink, with traces of pencil, [ca. 1893].

These two quick sketches are thought to be of Potter's pet rabbit, Benjamin.

12. *Capital letters "T," "A," "W."* Pencil, highlighted with ink, [ca. 1890s].

These amusing variations on Victorian ornamental alphabet letters may be related to a projected book. A similar drawing is in the Victoria and Albert Museum, London.

13. *Rabbit in Red Jacket Shoveling Snow.* Watercolor, January 1899.

In January 1899 Potter travelled (accompanied by a servant) to the Sussex seaside resort of Hastings to escape the cold weather in London. Although this drawing may have been executed earlier—perhaps several years before—it is inscribed on the back "To Mrs. White from Miss Potter in remembrance of a pleasant time in Hastings January 1899."

14. *Two Bunnies in a Sledding Accident.* Watercolor, 1894.

A nearly identical version, used for a one-of-a-kind greeting card, is in the Free Library of Philadelphia.

15. *Transformation Watercolor of Rabbit with Basket of Carrots.* Watercolor, 1895.

Toy pictures—complicated and often double-sided artworks in which flaps or openings reveal parts of the design—form a rare but exceptionally charming aspect of Potter's art. In this elaborate example, the front side shows a rabbit bringing carrots to a party, and a hinged door opens to disclose another rabbit welcoming guests. The reverse displays the same scene, as viewed from the inside of the house, in which the partying rabbits are already enjoying a head of cabbage.

16. *Rabbit outside Potting Shed.* Ink and wash, [ca. 1890s].

17. *Rabbits in Potting Shed.* Ink and wash, [ca. 1890s].

The realistic setting in these drawings was that of the potting shed at Bedwell Lodge, a country house in Hertfordshire that the Potter family rented in the summer of 1891.

18. *A Happy Christmas*. Watercolor, [ca. 1890s].

This depiction of rabbits eating their Christmas dinner is probably related to *The Rabbits' Christmas Party*, a series of six watercolors in which a group of rabbits, dressed in blue coats, gather for the traditional British festivities, complete with mistletoe, dinner, dancing, and games.

ILLUSTRATIONS

Throughout the 1890s, for her own amusement and for the amusement of others, Beatrix Potter created inventive illustrations of fairy tales, contemporary children's literature, and traditional rhymes. The subjects, drawn from her reading, included Cinderella, Alice in Wonderland, and "The Owl and the Pussy Cat." Potter's artistic style, already mature, showed the influence of the well-known book illustrators Kate Greenaway, Walter Crane, and Randolph Caldecott. It also reflected the state of color printing when her works began to be reproduced as greeting cards and in gift volumes. For chromolithography, Potter adapted her palette and technique to produce images suitable for a cheap and often imprecise method. She used a fairly dry brush, which gave her a precise line, especially good for rendering the fur of small animals. Later, as she began to illustrate her own tales of imaginary doings in the animal world in the Peter Rabbit books, her style changed to admit the use of color wash, to take advantage of technological improvements, in particular the three-color printing process.

19. *Cinderella's Coach.* Wash, 1899.

The Cinderella tale appealed greatly to Potter. Late in life she wrote her own version of the story, but much earlier she made several illustrations in which, typically, the coach is pulled by rabbits in place of the traditional horses. This watercolor was presented by Potter to her fiancé, Norman Warne, who was also her editor and publisher. Potter and Warne were engaged briefly during the summer of 1905 before Warne died unexpectedly, at the age of thirty-seven, on 25 August 1905.

20. Frederic E. Weatherly. *A Happy Pair.* London: Hildesheimer and Faulkner, [1890].

This is one of the few extant copies of the first published book to contain illustrations by Beatrix Potter. In 1890, the London gift book and greeting card publisher Hildesheimer and Faulkner, which had accepted the six watercolor illustrations she had sent them, asked her for more. They used her designs on Christmas and New Year's cards and in *A Happy Pair,* a thin volume of poems by the now-forgotten Victorian versifier, Frederic E. Weatherly. The chromolithographed cover and illustrations, authorship otherwise unidentified, are signed with Helen Beatrix Potter's initials, "H. B. P."

21. *Comical Customers at the New Stores of Comical Rhymes and Stories*. London: Ernest Nister, [ca. 1895].

Comical Customers was illustrated by several artists, including Louis Wain, William Foster, G. Henry Thompson, and Beatrix Potter. Potter's nine drawings accompany Clifton Bingham's verses "A Frog he would a fishing go," and are similar to those found in a picture letter she wrote the previous year to Eric Moore about a frog called Mr. Jeremy Fisher. In 1905 Mr. Fisher appeared in his own story, *The Tale of Jeremy Fisher*.

22. *"The Owl and the Pussycat."* Autograph manuscript with pencil and ink illustrations. 1897.

Edward Lear was, not surprisingly, one of Potter's favorite writers. This booklet manuscript of his famous poem contains eight illustrations, some of which may be judged among the great Victorian depictions of connubial happiness. On the first leaf is a note of presentation to Potter's cousin, Molly Gaddum:

March 6, 97

My dear Molly,

I have drawn you some pictures of the owl and the pussycat. It is very odd to see an owl with hands, but how could he play on the guitar without them? I remain your affectionate cousin, B

23. *"Two Little Mice Sat Down to Spin."* Autograph manuscript with watercolor illustrations. March 1892.

Potter produced various drawings and watercolors of spinning mice, some with two mice, some with three, some with ten. She hoped to publish an illustrated booklet of the traditional rhyme "Three little mice sat down to spin," but the idea never came to fruition.

24. *Three Blind Mice*. Ink and pencil, [ca. 1892].

25. *Mice Dancing*. Ink and pencil, [ca. 1892].

26. *Guinea Pig Gardeners*. Pencil, ink, and watercolor, 1899.

27. *"Cecily Parsley lived in a Pen . . . ."* Autograph manuscript with ink and watercolor illustrations, 1896.

28. *Cecily Parsley's Nursery Rhymes*. London: Frederick Warne and Co., [1922]. Signed by Potter on the title-page.

The illustrated manuscript "Cecily Parsley lived in a Pen" (apparently the earliest of several versions), the sketches of mice, and the watercolor of *Guinea Pig Gardeners* were executed in the 1890s. All are early versions of illustrations which were published in 1922 in *Cecily Parsley's Nursery Rhymes*, Potter's second collection of traditional nursery rhymes.

29. *Pussy-Cats*. Double-sided watercolor on board. May 1895.

This double-sided watercolor was created as a gift for Noel Moore, whose mother had been Potter's governess. One side shows a pussycat house, and the other a fish cart driven by a goat, with Mrs. Pussycat and her kittens observing a tradesman cat weighing fish. A small ink version of the central image occurs in Chapter XXI of *The Fairy Caravan* (1929).

30. *The Fairy Caravan*. By Beatrix Heelis ("Beatrix Potter"). [Ambleside:] Copyright of the Author, 1929.

The copy displayed is one of the 100 copies of *The Fairy Caravan* issued for the author's use and to secure British copyright. On page 196 appears an illustration based on the double-sided watercolor of a pussycat house which Potter gave to Noel Moore in 1895.

PETER RABBIT

The story of Peter Rabbit was first told by Beatrix Potter in a September 1893 illustrated letter to Noel Moore, the five-year-old son of her former governess. Perhaps the most famous letter ever written to a child, it began: "My dear Noel, I don't know what to write to you, so I shall tell you a story about four little rabbits whose names were Flopsy, Mopsy, Cottontail and Peter." Peter, of course, was inspired by Potter's own pet rabbit of the same name, who was, she said, "good at tricks." In 1900, she decided to write a book for children and, after borrowing back the letter from Noel, rewrote the story in an exercise book, adding forty-two ink drawings and a color frontispiece. This manuscript, titled "The Tale of Peter Rabbit and Mr. McGregor's Garden, by H. B. Potter," was submitted to at least six publishers. None showed immediate interest, so Potter decided to have it printed at her own expense by the London firm of Strangeways. The first edition of *The Tale of Peter Rabbit*, privately printed, was in the author-illustrator's hands by 16 December 1901. Potter gave copies as Christmas presents to family and friends, and sold others for a shilling each (plus two pence for postage). The demand was sufficient for a further 200 copies to be printed.

One of the publishers who had considered the manuscript, Frederick Warne and Co., had, by this time, agreed to publish the book commercially. At Warne's request—they wanted all the illustrations to be in full color—Potter made new watercolors of the previously reproduced line drawings. She remained adamant that children's books should be affordable and fit comfortably in small hands, so that when Warne's edition appeared in October 1902, it took the form of a tiny volume priced at one shilling in paper boards, one shilling and six pence bound in cloth. *The Tale of Peter Rabbit* was an immediate success. By the end of the year Warne had gone back to press twice and 28,000 copies were in print. Since then, the book has sold millions of copies and been translated into more than thirty languages, including Latin, Japanese, and Icelandic. Potter said that she "never quite understood the secret of Peter's perennial charm." But children and adults alike have responded to the powerful appeal of a tale that celebrates mischief and rule-breaking and allows for vicarious pleasure in a naughty rabbit's adventures.

While *The Tale of Peter Rabbit* inaugurated the twentieth century, the actual rabbit that inspired it did not. Peter Rabbit died—just four days after Queen Victoria—at the end of January 1901. In one of the privately printed copies of the book Potter wrote:

> In affectionate remembrance of poor old Peter Rabbit, who died on the 26th. of January 1901 at the end of his 9th. year. He was bought, at a very tender age, in the Uxbridge Road, Shepherds Bush, for the exorbitant sum of 4/6.... whatever the limitations of his intellect or outward shortcomings of his fur, and his ears and toes, his disposition was uniformly amiable and his temper unfailingly sweet. An affectionate companion and a quiet friend.

31. Statement for *The Horn Book Magazine*. Autograph manuscript, [November 1940].

Almost forty years after the appearance of *The Tale of Peter Rabbit*, Bertha Mahony Miller, the founder and editor of *The Horn Book Magazine*, asked Potter to retell the story of how *Peter Rabbit* came to be written. In this account, which was published in the magazine under the title "The Strength that Comes from the Hills," Potter said:

> It seems a long time ago and in another world that Peter Rabbit was written. Though after all the world does not change much in the country, where the seasons follow their accustomed course— the green leaf and the sere—and where Nature, though never consciously wicked, has always been ruthless. In towns there is change. People begin to burrow underground like rabbits. The

lame boy for whom Peter was invented more than forty years ago is now an air warden in a bombed London parish.

I have never quite understood the secret of Peter's perennial charm. Perhaps it is because he and his little friends keep on their way, busily absorbed with their own doings. They were always independent.

32. *The Tale of Peter Rabbit.* [London: Privately Printed, 1901].

The Tale of Peter Rabbit, Beatrix Potter's first book, was privately printed in an edition of 250 copies and was ready in time for Christmas 1901. Although the volume was a herald of twentieth-century children's literature in both content and illustration, one aspect of its manufacture was entrusted to a major figure in late-Victorian book production. Carl Hentschel, Aubrey Beardsley's preferred engraver, supplied, by means of the new three-color process, the frontispiece of Peter ill in bed, being served camomile tea by his mother, Mrs. Rabbit. (Warne's first published edition of 1902 was, in turn, produced by another important Victorian bookmaker, Edmund Evans, the celebrated color printer who had worked for Randolph Caldecott, Kate Greenaway, and Walter Crane.) This copy is inscribed to Potter's cousin, "For Miss Hoyer from Beatrix Potter Jan. 1902."

33. *Beatrix Potter's The Tale of Peter Rabbit: A New Printing from the Original Line-Blocks made for the First Private Edition of 1901, Introduced by Maurice Sendak.* Kingston, N.Y.: Battledore Ltd., 1995.

The thirty-four prints in this portfolio are restrikes from the original printing-blocks made for the 1901 first edition. As Sendak points out in his introduction, although the production of the later Warne edition was superior, these first black-and-white drawings have a "dash" and energy which was inevitably lost in the more polished colored versions. The private printing also included two images, reprinted here, which were removed from later editions of *The Tale of Peter Rabbit:* a group portrait of Peter and his sisters, and a picture of Mrs. McGregor serving up Peter's father in a pie. Sendak also notes Potter's similarity to Jane Austen in her steady view of her own talents, in her firm commitment to her own style, and even in some artistic themes. This is one of 250 sets signed by Maurice Sendak and by Iain Bain, who produced and designed the edition.

34. *The Tale of Peter Rabbit.* [London: Privately Printed], February 1902.

The positive response to the first privately printed edition of *The Tale of Peter Rabbit* led Potter to have her printer, Strangeways, produce a further 200 copies which were issued with a title-page dated February 1902. This second printing, called by some a second edition, by others a second issue—the bibliographical status is somewhat uncertain—had a slightly different binding and incorporated a few minor changes in punctuation and text. Shown here is a copy inscribed by Noel Moore, "Noel Moore. The idea of this book originated in a letter written to me by Beatrix Potter. 1893."

35. *The Tale of Peter Rabbit.* London: Frederick Warne and Co., [1902].

Frederick Warne, among the publishers which had been offered the original manuscript, agreed to publish *The Tale of Peter Rabbit* just prior to the appearance of the first privately printed edition. They believed the book would benefit commercially if all the illustrations were reproduced in color. Potter drew a set of new watercolors, creating what are now iconic images which show Peter in his famous blue coat. The 8,000 copies (in two bindings) of *Peter Rabbit* which Warne published on 2 October 1902 sold out at once. This copy of what is commonly termed the "first trade edition" is inscribed by Noel Moore, who refers to Potter's letter which contained the original story: "Noel Moore. See her letter dated to me in 1893."

36. *Peter Rabbit.* Doll, [ca. 1905].

Soon after the appearance of *The Tale of Peter Rabbit*, Beatrix Potter created several Peter Rabbit toy animals based on her own designs. Well aware of the commercial possibilities of a huggable Peter (after all, this was the era of Teddy Bear incunabula), Potter wrote to her publisher as she worked: "I have not got it right yet, but the expression is going to be lovely; especially the whiskers— (pulled out of a brush!)." This Peter Rabbit, with his blue coat, whiskers, and wise and experienced expression, was most likely one of the samples made by Potter, or for her, to obtain a patent to protect her rights.

37. *Mrs. Rabbit with Basket and Umbrella.* Watercolor on silk, [ca. 1910–1920].

38. *Mrs. Rabbit Buttoning Peter's Coat.* Watercolor on silk, [ca. 1910–1920].

Long after *The Tale of Peter Rabbit* first appeared in print, Potter continued to create artistic versions of the story. These examples are thought to be among the many she made to be sold to raise funds for various charities, including the National Trust.

39. *Peter Rabbit.* Autograph Christmas Card. Watercolor and ink. 1929.

Peter Rabbit is featured here in a patriotic mood, blowing a horn and holding a flag intended to be a Union Jack. The card's inscription, "A Merry Christmas to Joy Brownlow and the Windermere Girl Guides from Peter Rabbit and Beatrix Potter Dec 1929," explains the context. Groups of Girl Guides (the female counterpart to the Boy Scouts) enjoyed visiting Beatrix Potter at her home in Sawrey, and troops camped there in the summers.

ILLUSTRATED AND MINIATURE LETTERS

Between 1892 and 1912 Potter wrote illustrated letters to Noel and Eric Moore, the children of her former governess, Annie

Carter Moore. These "picture letters" to Noel and Eric, their sisters, and other delighted recipients contained lively details about the happenings in Potter's life and in the lives of her pets and other animals she encountered. Stories about Benjamin and Peter, Potter's pet rabbits, and characters such as Mr. McGregor and Jeremy Fisher appeared in picture letters, long before these now well-known names found their way, with Potter's illustrations, into print.

Potter's correspondence with children also took the form of miniature letters. Written from about 1905 until her marriage in 1913, these were styled as if from one character in her books to another or, on occasion, as if from a character to the actual child recipient. When receiving these letters, the children's knowledge of the stories in Potter's books would add to their appreciation of the content. The miniature letters formed their own envelopes when folded, and some were sent in a tiny mailbag made by Potter and inscribed "G. P. O."

40. Autograph illustrated letter to Noel Moore, 21 August [1892].

In this very early picture letter to Noel Moore, written more than a year before she sent him the story of Peter Rabbit, Potter tells and illustrates how her pet rabbit Benjamin Bouncer was transported to London in a basket. Concerned that Benjamin, Peter's "cousin," might want his freedom after his long trip, she wrote, "I have to lead him with a strap for fear he should run away into the fields."

41. Autograph illustrated letter to Eric Moore, 21 August [1892].

A companion to the adjacent letter written on the same day to Noel Moore, this missive to Noel's younger brother Eric begins with sketches and an account of Potter's pet mouse:

> Do you remember the little mouse you saw at Bolton Gardens. I have got another one with a white mark on its head. It is so tame that it will sit on my hand and eat hemp seeds. He was very ill once and I gave him some medicine and now he is quite well again.

On the inner pages are drawings of a field mouse, a duck and ducklings, and a fisherman next to a bridge. The final page— which has no text—contains pictures of a mouse ill in bed, a rabbit with an umbrella, and a squirrel gazing at three chirping birds. It is interesting to note that virtually all the images prefigure characters in Potter's books.

42. Autograph illustrated letter to Margaret Hough, 22 February 1905.

Not much is known about Margaret Hough and her brother John, but the correspondence between them and Beatrix Potter spanned several decades. Here, in an elaborate picture letter, Potter thanked Margaret for her photograph, which she has sketched hanging on the wall in a doll's house, being looked at by Hunca Munca, one of the protagonists in the recently published *The Tale of Two Bad Mice*. Potter confesses, ". . . I like writing lots of stories, but the pictures take such a time to finish!"

43. *The Tale of Two Bad Mice*. London: Frederick Warne and Co., 1907. Later edition (first published 1904).

Tom Thumb and Hunca Munca are the husband and wife pair in *The Tale of Two Bad Mice* who do quite a bit of mischief in the house inhabited by the dolls Lucinda and Jane. The doll's house in the story was based on the one built by Potter's editor Norman Warne for his niece Winifred, and photographs were used to prepare the illustrations.

44. Three miniature autograph letters: "Benjamin Bunny," "Peter Rabbit," and "Josephine Rabbit," to Jack Ripley. 1908–1909. Accompanied by two envelopes and a postcard photograph of Potter's pet rabbit, Benjamin, inscribed on the reverse: "With Benjamin Bunny's love to little Jack Ripley, he has got a very little hand, full of kisses, so he writes very little letters Beatrix Potter Feb 26th 08."

Little is known about Jack Ripley except that he was the son of a breeder of polo ponies and that he received several miniature letters from Beatrix Potter. One was addressed to Jack in Argentina, where he might have accompanied his father on a business trip. The texts of the letters are as follows:

Master J. Ripley
Siddington Hall.

Dear Jackie

My cousin Peter's envelopes are a very inconvenient shape! I have only got room to say I hope you are very well, and there is going to

be another book [*The Tale of the Flopsy Bunnies* (1909)] about me and my family. It won't be ready till September, it will be called (but that is a secret at present) so no more until we meet again in September. I have grown up since you saw me last!
Benjamin Bunny

Master J. Ripley
Siddington Hall

Dear Mr Jackie,

I am obliged to you for sending me a lovely calendar like a rose. I have tasted it and I think it is made of paper. So I shall not eat any more of it, I shall hang it up in my rabbit hole!
Love from your friend
Peter Rabbit

Master J. Ripley
Siddington Hall

Dear Mr Jackie,

My son Peter has written to thank you for the roses, they will decorate my rabbit hole most elegantly, & I was in want of another calendar.
Jos. Rabbit
P. S. I had not room to write my name properly.
Josephine Rabbit

45. Miniature autograph letter: "Peter Rabbit" to "Benjamin Bunny," [ca. 1905–1910].

While some miniature letters were addressed to children, others served as communications between characters in Potter's books:

Master Benjamin Bunny
The Warren.
Dear Cousin Benjamin
I have heard that Mr McGregor is in bed with a cold, I have heard him sneezing half a mile off. Will you meet me at 6 this evening in the wood outside the garden gate?
In haste yr aff cousin
Peter Rabbit

46. Two miniature autograph letters: "Tom Kitten" to "Mister Alexander B[rown]," January 1912, and "Josephine Rabbit" to "Mrs. Tiggy Winkle," [ca. 1905].

In the second letter, Peter Rabbit's mother, Josephine Rabbit, writes on a pressing matter to Mrs. Tiggy-Winkle, the hedgehog washerwoman in *The Tale of Mrs. Tiggy-Winkle* (1905):

Dear Madam,
Though unwilling to hurt the feelings of another widow, I really cannot put up with *starch* in my pocket handkerchiefs. I am sending this one back to be washed again. Unless the washing improves next week I shall reluctantly feel obliged to change my laundry.
Yrs truly Josephine Rabbit.

47. *The Tale of Benjamin Bunny.* London: Frederick Warne and Co., 1904. With miniature autograph letter: "Joseph Rabbit" to Miss Daune Rashleigh, [ca. 1913].

Daune Rashleigh, who was evidently another child-fan of Potter, carefully preserved this miniature letter in her first edition of *The Tale of Benjamin Bunny*:

Miss Daune Rashleigh
Kaikoura
Malvern Wells

Dear Miss Daune

I am writing for Miss Potter, because Miss Potter is busy drawing Pigs; and she has taken such a long time to answer yur nice letter. It was funny about the 6d on the hills. I would eat your lobelia if I got into your garden! I am Miss Potter's rabbit, I shall be 8 years old next May.
your loving friend
Joseph Rabbit.
'Peter' was before my time!

The pigs "Joseph Rabbit" refers to were those in *The Tale of Pigling Bland,* the twentieth in the series of Peter Rabbit books, published in 1913.

AFTER PETER RABBIT

Within two years, *The Tale of Peter Rabbit* was followed by *The Tale of Squirrel Nutkin* and *The Tailor of Gloucester.* Both were enthusiastically received by critics and public alike. Further titles followed, many reflecting Beatrix Potter's growing love of the English lakes where she frequently vacationed with her family. In all, between 1901 and 1913, she wrote and illustrated a total of eighteen "Peter Rabbit Books." The series benefited from a happy collaboration with publisher Frederick Warne and Co., in particular with her editor, Norman Warne. In 1905 she was briefly engaged to Norman Warne, despite her parents' objections to a union they considered beneath her. Sadly, Warne died within weeks. In the period of grief which followed, Potter created some of her best work, including *The Tale of Mr. Jeremy Fisher*, *The Tale of Jemima Puddle-Duck*, *Ginger and Pickles*, and *The Tale of the Flopsy Bunnies*.

Income from her books allowed Potter to buy Hill Top Farm in Near Sawrey in the Lake District in 1905. Other purchases of land followed. In 1913, at age forty-seven, and again against her parents' wishes, she married William Heelis, a country solicitor, and settled down as a country woman and successful sheep breeder. Only seven books were published during the remainder of her life; these were drawn, for the most part, from fragments of writing and art done decades earlier. In 1929 *The Fairy Caravan*, a lengthy and autobiographical story, was published in Philadelphia and issued privately in England. It was followed by *Sister Anne* (1932) and *Wag-by-Wall*, the last issued posthumously.

The earliest of the "little books," based on picture letters Potter had written for real children, were her gateway to intellectual and personal freedom. Her later books were done to please herself. "I cannot work to order," she once wrote, "and when I had nothing more to say I had the sense to stop."

48. *The Tailor of Gloucester.* [London: Privately Printed], December, 1902.

Beatrix Potter's second book, *The Tailor of Gloucester*, was, like her first, originally issued in a privately printed edition. She had doubts, even after the success of *The Tale of Peter Rabbit,* that her work was saleable, and worried that the story—based on real events but enhanced with a Christmas setting—was too long and too full of "old rhymes" to appeal to children. Frederick Warne, however, was optimistic, and published it a year later, in 1902, although with a shortened text and with only nine of the sixteen illustrations. *The Tailor of Gloucester* remained Potter's favorite among her own books.

49. *The Tailor of Gloucester.* [London: Privately Printed], December, 1902.

The privately printed edition of *The Tailor of Gloucester* included a cover illustration which was dropped from all the subsequent commercial editions. This copy is inscribed to Potter's cousin, "For Miss Hoyer from Beatrix Potter, Jan 16, 1903."

50. *Studies for The Pie and the Patty-Pan.* Watercolor, ink and pencil, [ca. 1905].

These studies for *The Pie and the Patty-Pan* (1905) shed light on Beatrix Potter's working methods. She first prepared sketches—sometimes large numbers of them—which were often partially inked in or touched with watercolor. From these, more finished illustrations were derived, the final versions almost perfect in execution. As with many of Potter's books, the settings and characters in *The Pie and the Patty-Pan* are based on actual places and real animals. The scenes are drawn from Lakefield Cottage in the village of Sawrey, and Duchess, the dog who is invited to tea by the cat Ribby, is based on two Pomeranians which belonged to Mrs. Rogerson, one of Potter's neighbors.

51. *The Tale of Mrs. Tiggy-Winkle.* London: Frederick Warne and Co., 1905.

Mrs. Tiggy-Winkle, the hedgehog "clear starcher" who did the laundry of other animals, probably originated in an old Scots washerwoman encountered by the Potters during their holidays in the Highlands. The story was written in 1901 in Lingholm, near Keswick, to which Beatrix Potter returned in 1904 when preparing backgrounds for the illustrations. To give the title character the right look, Potter worked from her own pet hedgehog (called, of course, Mrs. Tiggy-Winkle) and from an artist's lay figure, "dressed up . . . for convenience of drawing the clothes."

52. *The Story of a Fierce Bad Rabbit.* Autograph manuscript with watercolor illustrations, [1906].

"At the beginning of 1906 when working on *The Tale of Mr. Jeremy Fisher,*" writes Leslie Linder, Potter "was also planning some stories for very young children. Each story contained fourteen pictures and fourteen pages of simple text. The pictures and text were arranged in pairs and were in panoramic form, mounted on a long strip of linen, and folded concertina-wise into a wallet with a tuck-in flap. Three stories were written in this form—*The Story of a Fierce Bad Rabbit, The Story of Miss Moppet,* and *The Sly Old Cat;* but only the first two were published." *The Story of a Fierce Bad Rabbit* was written specially for Harold Warne's daughter, Louie, who had told "Aunt Beatrix" that Peter was "much too good a rabbit," and she "wanted a story about a really naughty one!"

53. *The Story of a Fierce Bad Rabbit.* London: Frederick Warne and Co., [1906].

The first edition of *The Story of a Fierce Bad Rabbit* was issued in a "wallet" format which mimicked the folding panoramic manuscript. Shops were reluctant to stock this unusual production, which was considered too awkward for children to handle and too easily damaged. *The Story of a Fierce Bad Rabbit* and *The Story of Miss Moppet*, the only other works by Potter issued in this form, were therefore commercial failures, with the result that when both were reprinted in 1916, they appeared as ordinary books.

54. *Ginger and Pickles.* London: Frederick Warne and Co., 1909.

Ginger and Pickles is the story of Mr. John Taylor's shop in Sawrey, the village nearest to Potter's Hill Top farm. Although the book is dedicated to Mr. Taylor, the shopkeepers in the story are the cat Ginger and his terrier friend Pickles.

55. *The Tale of Mrs. Tittlemouse.* London: Frederick Warne and Co., 1910.

Potter's passionate interest in all kinds of creatures is evident in her illustrations for *The Tale of Mrs. Tittlemouse,* in which insects are prominently featured. The book contains the only appearance of a ladybug in her published work. This copy, in the variant deluxe binding, is inscribed to her cousin, "For Victoria [Wrigley] with love from cousin B. August 15th [19]10."

56. *Jemima Puddle-Duck.* Doll. [ca 1910]. Accompanied by photographs and by patent registration form, 17 June 1910.

This Jemima Puddle-Duck doll, made in England to secure patent rights, wears a bonnet and shawl sewn from Liberty of London fabrics printed at the cotton mills upon which the Potter family fortune was based. It is displayed with the photographs, taken from several angles, which were required for registration, and the registration form itself. It is interesting to note that the date of the document, 17 June 1910, follows the publication of *The Tale of Jemima Puddle-Duck* (1908) by more than a year and a half. In a related letter to Margaret Hough, Potter wrote, "I should like to send 'Jemima' because I have taken a great deal of interest in getting her made."

57. *The Tale of Pigling Bland.* London: Frederick Warne and Co., 1913. With two autograph letters to Barbara Ruxton, 6 November and 13 December 1913.

Potter worked on the illustrations for *The Tale of Pigling Bland* in the months prior to her marriage in October of 1913 to William Heelis. The story concerns two real pigs at her own Hill Top Farm, which is the setting for several illustrations. The book's color plates also include a rare self-portrait—Potter bending over the piglet Alexander. Barbara Ruxton and her sister were Potter's guests at the farm when she was working on these illustrations. In one of the pictures, Potter mistakenly drew a cockerel too high on the page in relation to the pig, Alexander. It was Barbara who suggested that a plant saucer be drawn under the bird. In gratitude Potter gave her this first edition, inscribed "for Barbara Ruxton with love from Beatrix Heelis." The first letter, which accompanied the book, was written shortly after her marriage. In the second, Potter writes of moving to Castle Cottage, her principal home for the rest of her life.

Nov. 6. 13
Bolton Gardens S.W.

My Dear Barbara

I am sending you the new book [*The Tale of Pigling Bland*] now, instead of writing at Christmas, because I happen to be in London, & I am posting my books off instead of carting them up to Sawrey. I *shall* be glad to get back on Monday; I had to come up to see my parents who are very old—so I only had a fortnight's honeymoon.

43

It was delightful at the farm, the autumn colors are lovely.

I haven't got one to spare for Gussie—hope she won't be jealous! You must promise to come & see me again someday—there will be spare bedrooms at one house or the other.

Yrs aff

"Peter Rabbit"

Nobody remembers to call me Mrs. Heelis

Dec. 13. 13
Hill Top Farm
Sawrey
Ambleside

My dear Barbara,

I was delighted with your nice little basket, it will certainly be useful—and constantly used. It will just do for holding card of darning worsted of various colours. Mr. Heelis walks through the toes of his stockings so it is lucky I like darning!

It is surprising you could do the basket work so firmly—very creditable altogether.

I have never had time to write, as I went away to Appleby, to my new relations, for Christmas, now I am very busy writing letters & trying to tidy things up before going back to London to see my parents. I hope it will be fine tomorrow for the journey, the roads are very slippy but not much snow, & bright sun. Taps & pumps frozen this morning, we have got caught with no sacking on them.

I am hoping to get settled in the Castle Cottage soon—it has been such an *awful mess*. The new rooms are nothing like built yet, & the old part has been all upset with breaking doors in the wall & taking out partitions.

Those front rooms, where you & Augusta slept are one long room now & the staircase is altered, & we are going to have a

bathroom—in the course of time—I think workmen are very slow. With love & wishing you a very happy New Year
I remain yrs aff.
Beatrix Heelis
Be sure to come & call when you are in the neighborhood again, any time of day, perhaps I am oftenest to be found in the mornings.

58. *The Fairy Caravan.* By Beatrix Heelis ("Beatrix Potter"). [Ambleside:] Copyright of the Author, 1929.

In the late 1920s, Alexander McKay, head of the Philadelphia publisher David McKay Company, asked Potter to produce a book for her American readers. The result was *The Fairy Caravan*, a story about a traveling circus invisible to humans, which had its origins in the never-published *The Tale of Tuppenny,* written as far back as 1903. Due to what she considered the "too personal—too autobiographical" nature of the material (which included many Lake District references), Potter chose not to have *The Fairy Caravan* appear in England. However, in order to secure copyright, a British "edition" was necessary. To accomplish this, a private version limited to 100 copies was issued: a hybrid consisting of sheets sent over from Philadelphia with the first eighteen pages replaced by new text and illustrations printed by the local Ambleside printer, George Middleton. On the title-page Potter's name is given—for the first and only time—as Beatrix Heelis, and there is no publisher's name or place of issue, only the words "Copyright of the Author." Displayed here is the copy inscribed to her former governess, Madeleine Douglas

Davidson, "For M. D. D. With love from Beatrix Potter." The text contains numerous manuscript annotations by Potter, some of them unusually intimate, relating to and modifying various passages and discussing animals in the book.

59. *"The Wanderings of a Small Black Cat."* Autograph manuscript, [ca. 1930].

The incident described in this sixteen-stanza poem occurred many years earlier to the father of one of Potter's child-friends, Lucie Carr. According to Leslie Linder, "It was while staying at Lingholm, near Keswick that the Potters became friendly with the Vicar of Newlands and his wife, and their two children, Lucie and Kathleen. As a Christmas present in 1901, Beatrix Potter gave Lucie a copy of her privately printed *Peter Rabbit* — inscribing it, 'To Lucie with love from H. B. P., Christmas 1901 — I should like to put Lucie into a little book.' This she did some four years later in *The Tale of Mrs. Tiggy-Winkle,* and no doubt it was during the long summer holidays which Beatrix Potter spent at Lingholm, that Lucie saw much of her, and then played with her pet hedgehog Mrs. Tiggy-Winkle." *The Tale of Mrs. Tiggy-Winkle* (1905) was dedicated to Lucie Carr. Betty Harris, to whom the manuscript is inscribed, was a Philadelphian who developed a close friendship with Potter during her nearly annual visits to England in the 1920s and 1930s.

60. Collection of Twenty-Five Beatrix Potter Books. London: Frederick Warne and Co., [1902–1930].

This set of the first editions published by Frederick Warne includes twenty-three volumes in the "Peter Rabbit" series, from *The Tale of Peter Rabbit* of 1902 to *The Tale of Little Pig Robinson* of 1930, plus two additional titles, *Apply Dapply's Nursery Rhymes* (1917) and *Cecily Parsley's Nursery Rhymes* (1922). For most of the books, Potter and her publisher deliberately chose a small size intended to be comfortable in a child's hands. The nearly uniform format is most apparent when the series is displayed together. Here the entire group is housed in a folding morocco box made by the Cottage Bindery.

61. *Wag-by-Wall.* Boston: The Horn Book, Inc. 1944.

Wag-by-Wall was written in 1909, but neither the original text nor a version intended for *The Fairy Caravan* had been published when, in the early 1940s, Potter reworked the narrative into a Christmas tale at the request of Bertha Mahony Miller. Miller intended to include *Wag-by-Wall* in *The Horn Book*'s 1943 Christmas issue, but instead saved the story for the twentieth anniversary number, which was published in 1944, the year following Potter's death. The book editions, issued by the publishing arm of *The Horn Book* in Boston (with woodcut "decorations" by J. J. Lankes) and by Warne in London, marked the beginning of Potter's posthumous career.